VIRGIL BAKER

HOW TO REACH ANYTHING

**The Ultimate Guide on How to Execute
Your Goals, Discover The Proven Strategies
on How to Make Your Visions A Reality**

Descrierea CIP a Bibliotecii Naţionale a României
VIRGIL BAKER
    HOW TO REACH ANYTHING. The Ultimate Guide on
How to Execute Your Goals, Discover The Proven Strategies on
How to Make Your Visions A Reality / Virgil Baker – Bucharest:
Editura My Ebook, 2021
    ISBN

VIRGIL BAKER

HOW TO REACH ANYTHING

**The Ultimate Guide on How to Execute
Your Goals, Discover The Proven Strategies
on How to Make Your Visions A Reality**

My Ebook Publishing House
Bucharest, 2021

VIRGIL BAKER

HOW TO REACH ANYTHING

MV Book Publishing House
Bucharest 2021

TABLE OF CONTENTS

INTRODUCTION

Goal setting is the process of deciding what you would like to accomplish and then make a plan to achieve the desired result. Now while everyone has goals and aspirations, not everyone knows how to achieve those goals.

Goal setting is a structured process. First you decide on a goal, then you create a plan to get to that goal and finally you put your plan in action. It is this final part of the process that presents the most problems for many people. They easily set a goal and even devise a plan to get there but hit major roadblocks when executing their plan.

This book is your know all guide to setting goals and creating successful strategies to achieve those goals. Topics covered here will take a look at both personal goals for individual success and business goals to improve your business rather than any aspect of personal life. While both types of goals have different purposes, the essential goal setting process presents no major differences.

In fact, the same goal setting formula and strategies work for personal as well as business goals. So without further ado, here is what you need to know about the strategy-to-execution process.

Chapter 1

Vision Vs Execution

What is the difference?

Vision is great. In fact, it is the starting point for all big things to come. But vision means very little unless executed.

What this means is that it is great to have a plan but simply having a plan cannot get things done. It hardly even acts as a catalyst anymore. Take the very common example of trying to lose weight. You know you need to work hard and put in a certain amount of effort to shed off the extra pounds.

If you fail to lose weight on a diet, then is the diet the problem or is it because you didn't follow through consistently? The vision was to lose weight and the execution required you to invest time, effort and a lot of will power into the process. Were you able to deliver?

Another way to look at the same is trying to expand your blog. If your blog isn't growing, is it because your marketing strategy is poor, your writing style not up to the mark or simply because you can't seem to create enough useful content? You may have the vision to create a blog with broad readership but do you have the strategy and execution to take it that far?

Now vision and execution are not exclusive to the business world, although almost everything written about the topic refers to entrepreneurs and leaders, but can apply equally well to everyday non- business like situations as well, as we have just seen. So while a lot of the examples in this book might sound like they have to do with good leadership qualities only, feel free to apply the same to your personal aims and goals in daily life.

The effort threshold

Going by this working title, let us assume that every goal demands a minimum work threshold. If you do not invest at least a certain amount of effort, you won't get results. Based on the nature of the goal, the effort required may vary but the rule remains that you need to be engaged in following thorough.

Now go back to the example of trying to lose weight. If getting in shape requires a minimum commitment of gruelling for 3 hours per week and you only do it for 2, you won't get the desired results. Likewise, if becoming a successful blogger demands you to put in 1,000 hours of productive effort and you only contribute 400, chances are you'll fail. So even with a good plan in place, results do not come unless the plan is followed through.

Once again, vision needs execution to deliver results.

Defining vision

A vision for personal goals could be for anything ranging from improving your health, mastering a culinary skill, becoming a better person or even becoming more sociable when in company. In fact, it could be anything that empowers you as a person or makes you feel like an achiever.

In terms of business, vision is the grand idea of where your company may go as an extension of where it is already.

A vision statement organizes your thoughts and distributes them to the company. The statement is often lofty and future-based but still needs to be organized and planned carefully. It is kind of like a roadmap which points out the direction you would like to follow.

It is very important to have a solid vision since it is basically the stepping stone for planning your business. Your vision statement should include all the following elements:

- **Finance** - how to fund your projects or sustain and support your business

- **Reputation** - among staff, competitor and clients

- **Service quality standards** – focus on making clients a priority

- **Growth** - a plan on how to inprove locations, get more customers, expand inventory and innovate.

- **Passion** - articulating your dreams and hopes for the business

- **Sustainability** - determining your financial and environmental sustainability

Essentially your vision will provide the groundwork or blueprint before you go onto the execution phase.

Defining execution

If vision defines your goals then execution gets you to those goals. The success of any individual or business organization relies on its potential to convert a plan into reality. People who follow through putting their plan into action with a solid strategy often achieve those goals. Businesses that take on a logical and disciplined approach to doing things use many different techniques to convert their ideas into outcomes.

A word of caution - Execution is never perfect from the start so be ready to face obstacles along the way. No matter how solid your idea may sound to you, you need to realize that the path to getting that idea executed and achieving results will be a constant work in progress. There really is no way that you or anyone else on your team can know from the get-go what the end result will look like.

Your part in all of this is to make sure that actions are continuous and that change is welcome rather than spending time in the planning phases.

Some common pitfalls to avoid (especially in business scenarios) along the way can include the following:

- Spending too long on the planning phase

- Wanting to implement all phases at once

- Making money a priority in the project, and not the project itself

- Allowing personal emotions to keep others from helping

- Acting alone and not consulting with the team

Bringing the two together

Any successful entrepreneur will tell you that ideas are worthless without execution. Anyone who has ever attained their goals will also tell you the same. That is why the two need to be brought together so that results get produced. However, there is an entire process from vision to execution which we will look at very briefly here and in greater detail elsewhere. Step by step is the way to go.

In essence, **vision** is only the big idea behind every good or great plan. What it needs for it to have an effect is a **strategy**, by which it can be implemented. Now strategy is what you will follow to achieve that big idea.

By comparison, vision is a where and what while strategy is a how. Both vision and strategy are indispensable and missing either leaves you without direction and the capability to manage effectively.

Once you have a vision and strategy in place, the next step is **communicating** your idea and implementation plan to others. It is only when the plan is communicated to others that it can be effectively followed and executed. This holds true wherever a team is involved. You may be a gym teacher, a health guru, a motivational speaker or a businessman, you need to communicate your ideas well.

Once your vision has been communicated to others, it is time to take some **action**. And it is not only you that needs to act alone, but everyone on the team needs to do so too.

Let's say that everyone involved in a project decides to act. So what's next? This is important as it involves going back and **reviewing** whatever you have done so far. Successful individuals and organizations keep a close tab on the progress being made and how much work still remains. So, reviewing not only helps you with assessing progress but also charting the way forward.

It also ties in to **accountability** where you not only hold yourself but also your co-workers, colleagues, students or employees accountable to your vision and the actions that anyone has taken to get there. Accountability also paves the way for corrective action, if required.

If you can get through all these guidelines, then you have successfully executed your vision and no longer have an execution problem. However, the process is not as basic or simple as described here. After all, this entire book is dedicated to the power of execution so there's a lot more to come.

Chapter 2

Execution without Intention

Why Good Strategies Fail

Executing an idea can be very difficult which is why ultimately not every good idea becomes an instant hit. Sometimes, people decide not to do anything about their ideas and ideas get forgotten. Other times it can be external factors like lack of knowledge or mismanagement that kills off an idea before anything can happen.

But external factors aside, here we will look at aspects which are under your control and mismanagement on your part may be doing more harm than good.

The problem of under communicating

We already touched upon the importance of effective communication earlier, so let's elaborate that thought a little here. The problem remains that most leaders tend to under communicate by a huge factor.

However, the issue is that those who follow by example don't get it after a few times. There is so much communication going on all the time that your particular message can easily get lost in all that garble.

Many leaders tend to under-communicate their vision and strategy which means that their vision never makes it to the execution stage. If you want to communicate more effectively, you need to keep practicing your speech over and over again, as nothing beats relentless practice when learning new skills.

An important consideration here- do not be a stickler for simply saying it "verbally". Turn to other means of communication by saying it in person, on the phone, in an email, via video conferencing and also in meetings.

Lack of team involvement

So even if you are saying it enough times, are you sure that everyone can hear your message? This brings us to another reason why good strategies often fail.

Any business, whether small, mid-sized or large needs everyone to be on board. The same goes for non-business scenarios as well. Despite having the best plan on paper, execution can go out the window if all departments of the business are not involved. This is because the execution process needs contribution from every department so it needs to be a coordinated effort.

Remember that you cannot execute strategy alone. Do not undermine the size of your team when it comes to executing the plan. If you have a team of 6, things are fairly easy. Expand that number to 60 and things start getting trickier. Often strategy leaders do a great job of gaining support from their immediate colleagues and direct reports but do not present equally impressive results of securing similar support from others.

Many large companies view strategy as an annual activity conducted by an elite group of people who sequester themselves in a conference room. In smaller organizations the same comes as an edict from above on which employees must act.

But because execution of the strategy demands action it requires specific people to carry it out. Lack of such involvement can easily become the cause of strategy failure. When employees are not given the chance to question high level strategy, it can spell trouble for the company. Instead of isolating certain demographics, get the communication going through a conversation thread that involves everyone in the organization.

Involving team players early on will make the communication component of the process so much easier. And as seen earlier, communication is key to making sure that a strategy takes off and delivers results.

Too many times plans do take off with a blast only to see communication dwindle gradually as everyone returns to business as usual.

Poor decision making

Company success and failure are dictated by decision making. The same also applies when you think about achieving personal and not business goals. Among these, poor decision making can kill a good strategy if people in the organization do not see it as a source of strategy failure.

Given a directive of too many goals can create a situation where everything becomes a priority. In this situation nothing really gets accomplished but projects do remain pending. Given this scenario, it is important for business owners to know how to select, prioritize, edit and delete decisions.

If you are working on a personal goal like boosting confidence, developing leadership qualities, saving money, eating healthy or something similar, you will also need to make the right decisions. Some things you will have to be a stickler for while others you will need to forego completely. Pick and choose your options wisely. So whether a decision is made solo or is team based, it is important to make sure that you have a process where warning signals can be detected should you need to revisit your decision.

Remember an earlier reference to work in progress? Well, this is where you need to have the flexibility to make adjustments and improvise according to the demands of the situation.

Hiring the wrong people

Another good reason why a perfectly workable strategy doesn't work is because you hand it to the wrong person to execute. Often times, implementing a new strategy involves hiring or promoting an employee specifically tasked with executing that particular strategy.

But if you get the hiring wrong, then the strategy fails as well, or at least appears to do so. And because hiring is a difficult process, people just dump the strategy rather than go through the entire hiring process again.

Insufficient data or overly complex plans

Both these factors make up for poor communication. If a plan is based on wrong assumptions due to insufficient data or even misunderstood data then the drive towards execution will be a disaster from the start. A relatable example would be miscalculating financial estimates or even the number of people required for executing the plan.

An example of a personal goal could be something like wanting to travel to certain destinations without laying out an itinerary or budgeting your travel costs properly.

Likewise if a plan is too difficult to explain to others, how can you hope for effective communication and the desired result? When plans are not effectively capable of being explained given their complexity, team members cannot be expected to carry them out as intended.

A plan that has too many contingencies or restrictions will not only become too hard to follow let alone implement. Another reason why perfectly good strategies fail to take off.

Expecting results too soon

When you implement a strategy you need to give it time to produce results. If the results do not come quickly enough, don't start to tinker with the strategy.

There is often a lot of excitement at the beginning of a process followed by a decline in interest and a return to everyday business. To keep things going in momentum, try not to ditch or change the strategy. Instead your focus should be on preventing a loss of momentum.

Avoid changing the plan too much or too frequently as this can easily lead to losing credibility with employees or other team players. Changes should be gradual or even iterative rather than dramatic. Having said that, this does not apply to when there are clear cut signs of warning and you need to move quickly to tweak your plan accordingly.

In practice, successful execution is that which adapts to situations that emerge. Successful execution evolves and an organization's sustainability depends on its willingness and ability to adapt.

Chapter 3

Strategic Execution Part 1

The Planning Phase

Strategy execution is much like going on a trip towards a planned destination. Time for another example.

Consider going on a weekend trip, but first you need to make some arrangements. You need to decide on a destination, check the weather and road conditions, estimate travel time and decide how many stops you may need to make on the way. Then there are the unexpected consequences to consider such as road work, detours and others that may delay you getting to your destination. Once you reach your destination, you will have successfully executed all the planning into delivering results.

Earlier on, we touched upon the different steps of strategy-to- execution with a promise of more details to follow. Now we will look at that topic in a little more detail explaining the step by step process.

A successful strategy-to-execution process provides a structured approach to clarifying, communicating, implementing and managing strategy. The goal of the entire process is to make sure that you know where you are so you can determine where you need to go. This gives you a baseline to work from.

This first part of strategy execution deals with all the steps that go into setting up the stage for taking action.

1. Strategy planning

The journey of any successful execution begins with strategy planning. This component is important as it comes before taking any action.

This planning component needs to consider all issues ranging from the big and small steps the company needs to take to get to its goals, the framework they will use to keep on track along with the structure for strategy reporting and the frequency of strategy meetings.

If you look at it historically, corporate history is littered with businesses that experienced immense growth stalls only because they followed strategies built on wrong assumptions or a need of clarity.

The goal of successful strategic planning is to come up with a strategy that defines clear goals, while staying away from misaligned or ambiguous ones.

For personal goals, you still need to plan ahead, but perhaps in a different way. Say you would like to volunteer more in the upcoming year. This will require you to schedule the days and hours you would like to donate, the type of volunteer work you are interested in and any travelling to and from the location.

You need to plan this out in advance so it does not clash with your regular work-life balance and create a scenario where you are left feeling overwhelmed and unable to continue with your commitment.

2. Set clear goals

This stems directly from strategic planning where not having clear cut goals will make execution run amok. Whether you are an individual working for achieving personal goals or a business striving for successful expansion, your goals need to be defined clearly.

For instance, your goal may be as basic as learning a new language, where you may want to appreciate cultural diversity, or give yourself a competitive edge in career choices. You may want to do so as foreign languages open up the door to art, music, dance, fashion and cuisine, if any of those are your forte, or you may simply want to improve your communication skills. Whatever the reason, you need to have a goal in sight to work towards. Once you have the goal established you can then get to work to achieving it, which is all execution.

Likewise, in the business world, goal setting helps you organize your thoughts about what you want to achieve and allows you to come up with concrete steps that will help you get there. When you are clear on where you're going, it's a lot easier to make things happen. Having a goal is also motivating as you have a built-in finish line to work towards and you can celebrate when you reach it.

When talking about goals, whether personal or otherwise, these goals should be supportive of the overall strategy. For team members they should be tangible so that everyone involved get a sense of progression as they move along with the plan. Outlined goals should also be specific measurable, attainable and realistic while being timely.

Working with clear cut goals can also be beneficial in the sense that it can help weed out issues such as whether or not your plan is realistic with regards to any resource constraints. It also helps an organization establish whether they have the right individuals and skillset to execute the plan and also gives an idea of how well employees may have understood the company's overarching objectives.

As such goals become the basis of your ongoing tracking, reporting and performance management, every one of which is crucial in the implementation of successful execution.

Any goal that creates conflict or challenges resources will limit the execution success.

3. Communication

The manner in which businesses communicate and involve employees in latest strategies is crucial for promoting implementation. Statistics reveal that an approximate 65% of employees do not get their roles when different initiatives are introduced. The absence of an effective communication strategy can not only lower motivation but also spark a resistance to change.

Together, these factors can lead to inefficiencies in the system and raise the cost of execution.

Without communication team players can lose touch with the company's objectives and goals. Over time, both employee and entrepreneur may drift off course.

To make sure that the all departments stay in tune with the entrepreneur's vision and strategy, the team should gather frequently for different updates.

Ideally communication should start as early as the strategic planning itself. In fact, it should be a parallel to the process of planning. The communication component needs to be two way in the sense that you should be getting feedback about your strategy not only in the beginning but also as it unfolds.

There are quite a few different ways that you can facilitate this communication. For instance, regular meetings are one way to go.

- **Operational groups** could gather for a daily huddle at the start of the day to make sure that everyone is on the same page and updated.

- **Executive meetings** between key management personnel may be conducted regularly to assess the progress of the strategy implementation.

Interestingly enough, meetings can quickly disclose whether an organization has a strong culture of execution or not. For instance, if a meeting consists of a long presentation while other attendees sit quietly, unwilling to raise questions knowing that their own presentation will follow soon, then there is cause for concern. This scenario depicts an organization without a culture of execution and a place where even the best strategy may fail.

On the other hand, if a presentation is short and to the point with active participation by everyone present, with questions being answered and a common understanding that everyone is working on the same goals and timeline then this team is on the path to successful execution.

It is often very easy to fall into the trap of doing a great job of communicating at the start only to see people go back to business as usual. This also why planning communication ahead of time is important because it keeps the momentum up. At the same time, it is also important to engage key employees with targeted communication to win their support for the strategy.

Chapter 4

Strategic Execution Part 2

The Action Phase

Now, communication, as mentioned before kind of falls in both the planning as well as the action phase of the process. So let's stick to calling it a parallel between the two.

Once your strategy has been implemented and put into action, it is now time to track its progress and keep close tabs on how well it is performing.

1. Tracking progress

Integral to making sure that execution stays on track, it is important to keep a close eye on results. This means that having a goal isn't enough by itself. You also need to have some system of tracking your movement towards that target. In the absence of a frequent reminder of how you are doing, there is no way for you to know if the actions you take are working or not.

On the business front, since there's a whole team of people involved, entrepreneurs need to develop key indicators of performance that are measureable and monitored on a continuous basis. This will allow the executives to evaluate what is working and pursue these processes to enhance and promote performance. With declining results, businesses should decide what processes don't work and to make changes to prevent any further deterioration.

This point should also take task delegation into account. This means assigning the right job to the right person. Remember how hiring the wrong person for the job could bring down a perfectly good strategy? Well this is what you want to avoid.

Being mindful of a project, meeting individual and team deadlines is crucial to continuously move a project forward. This can include sharing regular updates which ensures that everyone on the team has a comprehensive understanding of the progress and how every person's input fits into the whole.

Even in non-business scenarios, tracking is essential for achieving goals. For instance, tracking progress helps everyone stay focused. A lot of people, not unlike businesses, fail to accomplish their goals not because they don't possess the skills but because they lose track of what they want to achieve. Businesses, on the other hand, may have the correct strategy but can bungle up due to the various reasons already mentioned earlier.

Another consideration for tracking progress is that if you don't track, you may end up focusing more on failures. It is natural for people to focus more on the negative side of things, so even after accomplishing something, a mishap may make you forget the earlier accomplishment. How many people have you known who have tried losing weight but then gained it all back again (or even weigh more than before!) simply because they got derailed from their initial diet plan for some reason? Why even think about other people when this may have happened to you yourself?

Likewise, business scenarios demand that all progress and setbacks be recorded vigilantly to weed out the mistakes from the accomplishments.

In a strictly entrepreneurial sense, tracking progress makes breaking bigger tasks into smaller steps much easier. A big presentation due in less than a week when broken down into smaller tasks such as research, task delegation, data analysis and choosing the medium for the presentation makes the strategic goals so much more attainable, realistic and less overwhelming.

Measuring progress in business

Looking at bottom line results in areas such as spending, sales or profits does not help understand how or why you reached those figures or how to improve performance.

One of the biggest benefits of measuring performance is that you identify areas where you may be struggling. If you have a master budget, conducting a monthly analysis will show you where your results do not meet your projections. Tracking may just be what you need to realize that your projections might have been too optimistic and that the performance did not live up to its expectation. Such measurements can help you pinpoint your weaknesses while letting you put checks where needed or take other measures to support your business.

On the other hand, tracking your sales, production, marketing and labor use helps you identify which aspects of your organization are doing well and which others need more attention.

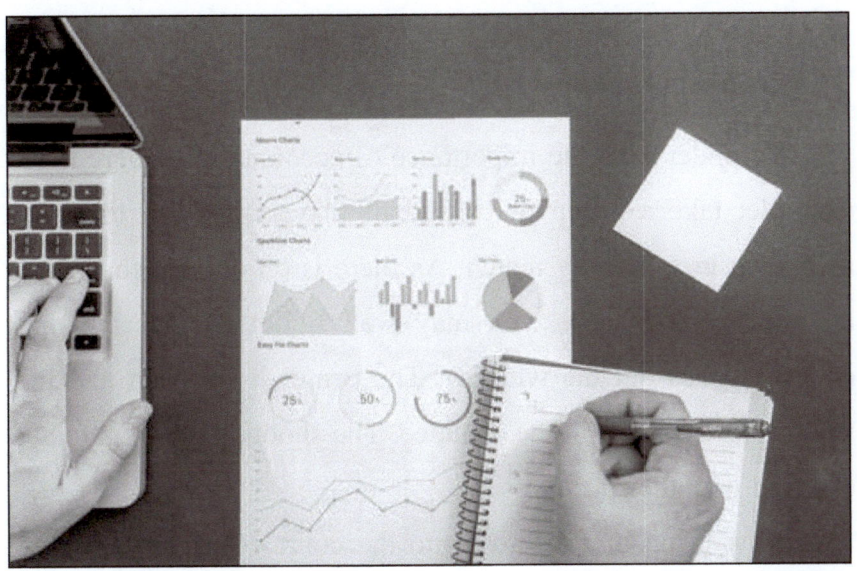

With tracking, employees are also able to see the progress the company makes. As such they may experience higher job satisfaction. Likewise, if they can see that their unit is struggling, then they might be motivated to work harder. So measuring results based on goals set for all employees and communicating the same to the staff on a scheduled basis helps keep the team motivated to do well whether they are surpassing those goals or struggling.

2. Accountability

To understand the importance of accountability, here is an example: take a group of basketball players and put them on their own in a friendly match. As there is on one watching and no one keeping score, you may well find that all sense and cohesion goes out the window. The center is up front and the small forward is off in the distance. The shooting guard is found chatting with the spectators.

Now bring in a referee onto the court who starts keeping score visibly. As most people would expect, the dynamics of the game will change instantly. Players would start playing positions they were assigned because now they are actually trying to perform well to win. The simple act of being observed and being held accountable for has made all the difference.

It is no different in the workplace setting. While holding people accountable certainly helps the business, it is only when accountability is made visible that real results are delivered.

As per the example, accountability was vaguely there with each player knowing their position and role, but it took a crowd of onlookers and a referee for them to start aiming for success in those roles. Employees at a business are much the same. With roles defined correctly, they will know what they need to do to succeed, but if their success is not marked or if the metrics are not visible or relevant, then accountability loses its impact.

When accountability is confusing or misapplied, consequences get watered down or never occur and people often miss the connection between results and recognition. Instead, reporting results to each other and holding each other accountable for achieving goals are key to successful execution.

Sticking to these basics (some may sound redundant but need emphasis at this stage) while holding your team accountable during the execution process:

Discuss and set up expectations: Clearly articulating expectation is not only mandatory but crucial to the organization's success in setting up accountability. Think about the basketball players from the previous example. Knowing their position and role in the game holds them accountable for any mistakes or gains made in their area.

Look for input: Looking for input engages team members in achieving goals. It gives them a chance to determine what works and establishes a vivid understanding of expectations.

Actively coach the team: Accountability and coaching go hand in hand. You need to know of any issues that arise to keep your team mindful and answerable to any action that they take.

Hold regular strategy reviews: Such strategy reviews, or call it communication is important to holding the team liable during the execution phase. As each step of the way is reviewed, everyone's performance becomes obvious and can give you a fairly predictable heads up on the progress of your strategy execution.

Chapter 5

How to Set Powerful Goals the S.M.A.R.T Way

Goal setting is important because it provides focus and allows you to work towards long range goals. In the meantime, you also get to learn how to get past short range obstacles along the way.

So goal setting is imperative for individuals, people, team players, coaches and corporations that wish to succeed. In fact it is for everyone who wants to set themselves up for success.

It can be anything basic from trying to lose weight, quit smoking, drinking enough water every day to more elaborate schemes like improving your savings, buying a house, travelling to certain destinations or even finding more time to spend with friends and family.

But even this process demands a bit of structure. Simply setting a vague or a broad goal and not knowing how to achieve it won't get you very far. So make sure that your goals are specific, measurable and realistic.

Plus, goals need to be something that motivate you. This means that it should be something that is important to you and there is a value in achieving it. If you have very little interest in the outcome or the goal is irrelevant, then it is not very likely that you will put in any real effort to achieve it. So motivation is key to achieving goals.

44

This makes goals relevant so set them according to priorities in your life. If you do not prioritize, then you may end up having too many goals leaving you too little time to devote to each one. But before we look at the rules for successful goal setting, here is what goals are all about:

Goals require action - In a nutshell, this point sums up the whole strategy-to-execution process. You have to take steps everyday which bring you closer to what you have in your mind.

Goals require deadlines - There has to be a time frame to deliver results.

Goals have a price - Not necessarily a monetary price for everyone, but goals will need you to invest time and effort and other things you can think of. If you're handling a business, then yes, money and funding is kind of a big one here.

Goals produce results - You have to be able to see progress along the way. If not then your goal is probably not clear enough or you do not have the skills or knowledge to make it happen.

Goals will challenge you - Nothing comes easy so yes, there will probably be some hiccups along the way. If you are not being challenged, then perhaps your goals are not big enough.

Goals require hard work - You need to be willing to work for what you want since no one else will do it for you. Pure and simple.

Once you keep these guidelines in mind when setting your goals, your goals should come out as realistic, tangible expectations. And to accomplish your goals, you should know how to set them.

Setting S.M.A.R.T goals

Setting S.M.A.R.T goals is a way to make sure that your goals are all the things that will help you get to where you want to go. Here is what each letter of the word SMART signifies:

Specific - Specific goals will give you direction, vague goals will lead you nowhere. Ambiguous goals produce ambiguous results whereas incomplete goals produce incomplete results. So when setting goals you need to be extremely clear to everyone including yourself as well as others. The goals should be specific by being exact, thorough and adept at answering questions instead of creating more.

Example: *I should spend more time with the kids* as opposed to *I will read the kids a story every night before bed or we will bake something together every Saturday.* The first example is too vague where you don't exactly know what you will do with the kids but the second becomes more specific identifying the kinds of activities you will share with the children. Now you have a plan to work with.

Measurable - This means including dates, amounts and numbers in your goals. Such figures will also give you benchmarks to measure your success. Evaluating progress is helpful in keeping you stay focused, meeting deadlines, and feeling the thrill of getting closer to attaining your goals.

Example*: I want to lose weight*- too vague. But when the goal becomes *I want to lose 40 pounds by August 15th*, it is more specific. You have just given yourself a measure of *how much* weight you would like to lose along with a *specific time*.

Attainable - Set an achievable goal that you can accomplish within the restrictions of money, time, skills, abilities, environment and other relevant factors. It may stretch your potential but still be possible to achieve. Also, when you set an attainable goal, you can also recognize previously missed opportunities or resources.

Example: *I want to make clean eating a habit for life.* But how do you attain this? *I want to eat cleaner by resisting junk food, planning meals before time and eating only whole foods.* By imposing some sensible restrictions on your dietary habits, you have made your goal more attainable.

Relevant - Your goals should be aligned with the direction you are following in life. This means keeping goals true to your purpose and not wasting time with irrelevant goals. Keeping goals relevant helps you align focus instead of frittering your time away.

Example: *I want to quit smoking* is too general. But when you set up the goal as *I want to quit smoking for improved health* it becomes relevant to why you want to do so. You may be doing so to improve heart health, respiratory health or even to reduce internal inflammation.

Time based - Every goal needs a delivery date so there is a time frame to work within. An important component of execution is that the strategy should have an end, a time in which you are aiming to accomplish it. For better management of a big goal, you can also break it into different parts and time frames. It also creates accountability along with a sense of urgency and achievement that will come.

Example: *I want to create a website to sell jewellery from my store* is just a simple goal. To make it smart, you need to work along the lines of *I want to create a website to sell jewellery from my store by January 31st. The website needs to be operational by the end of January so that so I can sell special valentines items before Valentine's Day. I will use a website development company to create the site.* Making a goal time specific may sometimes mean that you may need to outsource some tasks such as get a website development company to work on it.

Chapter 6

The Importance of Performance Coaching

By definition, performance coaching is a process where one individual facilitates the development and action planning of another. This can be done in a personal, organizational, professional or entrepreneurial context.

For instance, on a personal level, individuals can seek career coaching, emotional coaching, life coaching or even hypnotherapy among many others to achieve their goals.

Let's take a look at career coaching to start off. If you feel stressed or worried about your job security the coaching can help you cope with career changes, identify strengths and transferable skills, set realistic goals and develop a strategy to achieve the career you want. So if your goal is to learn new skills, change your role and give your career a boost, career coaching could help you get all that.

Likewise, if you feel like you need to manage emotions better to have a positive effect on your personal and organizational performance, you can look into emotion coaching to help you deal with change and conflict, gain a better understanding of responses to challenging situations and discover strategies to maintain positive and calm feelings.

Not only can individuals benefit from this type of coaching but even those who are team leaders, managers and those in a position of authority can use it to understand how motivation can have a positive impact on the productivity of their business and the performance of the employees.

So in a business context, performance coaching can improve a company's sales performance, enhance strategic thinking skills, and take the business to the next level. In fact, performance coaching is one of the many execution efforts to gauge individuals and companies towards achieving goals. Such coaching creates engagement to get things done.

Business corporations and team leaders of all sorts need to become good performance coaches to put their strategies into its execution phase. While there are many performance coaching methods out there, the most popular one is called the G.R.O.W. method.

Managers use this model to help their employees improve work performance, enhance problem solving skills, become better decision makers, acquire new skills and achieve their career goals. Once again an acronym like S.M.A.R.T, G.R.O.W also helps create the right context to help individuals transform their potential into peak performance.

What is the GROW coaching model?

The GROW model offers the coach a simple yet effective framework for goal setting and problem solving. The grow model works with a collaboration between a coach and a student to work towards achieving goals. As a leader the coach who may be a manager, a seasoned entrepreneur, a teacher or anyone in a similar position who can help a subordinate make better decisions, solve problems that may be holding them back learn new skills and otherwise progress ahead in their careers.

So how does GROW work towards achieving goals? Referring to an earlier example of taking a trip- first you decide where you want to go (Goal) then establish where you currently are (Reality). Then you look at all the possible routes to your destination (Options) before you establish the way (Will) to commit to making the journey and getting ready for any obstacles along the way. Let's break that down for easy understanding.

Goals - the most important part of the coaching phase is to define and agree on the goals to be achieved. Coaching begins with determining a relevant goal. This could be anything from, a developmental goal, a performance goal, a problem to tackle, or even a decision to make. Such individual goal setting is very important for execution as we have previously seen in earlier chapters.

If the goal seems overwhelming at the initial stage, try breaking it up into smaller fragments before moving on.

Identifying the goal:

- What do you want to accomplish?
- What would be the ideal outcome?
- How would achieving this goal benefit you?

Reality - reality lets you examine the current situation. If you want to proceed ahead with pursuing your goal, you need to be objective. Where execution is concerned, being realistic will let you remove many false assumptions from getting to your goal.

Reality is also all about gaining awareness of the present situation. Too often people try to solve a problem or reach a goal without considering their starting point. As such, they miss information they need in order to reach their goal effectively. Once there is a clear understanding of the situation, options can be explored for generating solutions to reach goals.

Identifying reality:

- Where do you stand in relation to your goal?

- What is an important factor in your success up till now?

- Why haven't you reached your goal already?

- What would you do better this time?

Options - After exploring the reality, focus can shift to considering the options. Options is when the individual explores and identifies ideas and solutions.

This step lets you determine what is possible and what is not. The coach does not make any decisions for you, but only guides you in the right direction.

Exploring options:

- What options do you have?

- What do you think you need to do next?

- What would you do different from before?

- How could you do it differently?

Will - this is the final component of the GROW model where the will or the way forward for execution is established. In other words, the action plan for the next step is determined.

The purpose of this final phase is to transition into the decision- making phase where you'll have to decide how you are going to achieve your goals. It is sort of like a commitment to specific actions to move towards the goal.

Exploring will:

- What resources could help you?

- Do you think there is anything missing?

- When will you start?

Applying the GROW model to businesses

In a traditional scenario, the GROW model coach only acts in the capacity of a facilitator assisting the client to choose the best alternatives without offering any advice or a direction.

When the same is applied to a business leader a few things may change. For instance, the team leader or executive may already have expert opinion to offer and it is part of their job to guide team members to make decisions that are best for the organization. Yet, at the same time it may be more proactive for people to draw conclusions for themselves rather than have these imposed upon them.

Example: *You have been at your job for the past year and would like to be promoted to team leader within the next two years*. Now this is a smart goal which is:

Specific - you want to be a team leader, moving ahead with your career

Measurable - from entry level to team manager

Attainable - because you already have some experience in the field

Relevant - to your career

Time bound - you're giving yourself a time frame to work within

Based on this SMART goal, you and your coach can brainstorm the additional skills you need to be successful in achieving your goal. You may need more experience of managing other people, dealing with overseas customers while also performing well in your current position.

You work with your coach to review available options such as lead a small team so you can get the experience you need. Perhaps you could spend some time in the overseas team. When establishing will or the way to move forward, your coach or manger could actually let you lead a small team on a minor project and mark your progress.

You have now set the wheels in motion towards achieving your goal - otherwise also referred to as strategy-to-execution.

Chapter 7

Why People Fail To Reach Their Goals

When people set up goals and fail to achieve them, there remains a known gap between *what the strategy says should be done* and *what actually gets done*. This is known as the execution gap and represents a scenario that is often caused by some very typical shortcomings.

On the personal front, these shortcomings stop you from achieving your individual goals while in the business world, the same can happen as a result of leadership flaws. Collectively, both scenarios present a want of clarity as well as action and fail when there are no metrics to measure success.

But in order for execution to be successful certain fundamental elements – as mentioned previously – need to be in place. While some you pursue diligently, others you need to avoid doing as they only widen the execution gap instead of bridging it. But when this doesn't happen then you need to stop doing the following to bridge the execution gap.

Stop making excuses

Excuses are easier to come up with than reasons for not doing something. They can vary from not having enough time to the economy being bad or the competition too high. In any case, excuses paralyze you and stop you from executing anything at all. Most excuses come up when you feel fearful, anxious, uncertain or just plain lazy. At these times it seems easier and safer not doing anything at all than tackling the goal you have set up for yourself. It makes you abandon your goal before you even start pursuing it.

Excuses also make you stop working for your goal. You may well keep saying that you want to achieve a goal but if you're not doing anything about it, then how can you hope to achieve anything? The basic understanding of the strategy-to-execution process is that action precedes results. If you want results, you must take action first.

Give your goal some meaning

To bridge the execution gap, it is very important that your goal means something to you. Now, this may start to sound redundant as the same has been mentioned elsewhere in the book as well. But because it is so important in the process of achieving a goal, it needs to be emphasized once again.

If you set a goal for the wrong reason, and chase after something you don't really need, you will not be driven to achieve it and the execution gap will never be bridged. So set yourself up for something that'll mean something for you.

Setting the wrong goal also takes motivation out of the execution equation. To make anything motivating, be it weight loss, expanding your social circle, setting a start-up business or expanding your clientele, you need to associate strong reasons to why you want to achieve something. These reasons will then become the driving force that fuel your motivation.

Another consideration in this regard is commitment versus convenience. With the right goal, you are highly likely to be 100% committed whereas anyone who isn't committed will opt out for convenience instead. Say, you have a scheduled gym session every week with a buddy who also gives you a ride there.

Now if you are committed to getting into better shape, building strength or just improving your overall health, you will attend that session every time no matter what. But if you find out that your gym buddy won't be attending this week, so you decide to skip the session as well. Here you have opted for convenience instead.

Since your friend won't be there to take you along, you find that it is too much work to get to the gym by bus and then back home. At this point just give yourself a little reminder that the goal is to get *yourself* in better shape, no matter what. Set the bar for commitment higher so it's not that easy to back off.

Stop trying your hand at everything

This ties in to setting your priorities straight and focusing on 0ne goal at a time. When you divide your attention, energy and focus into too many parts, you fail to hone your expertise and skills where they could flourish the most.

If you want to execute your strategy successfully, you need to know your strengths. You need to know what you are good at, passionate about and most driven to do. Investing in the wrong goal will only stop you mid-way without ever being able to bridge the execution gap.

Think of examples of highly successful individuals who excel at what they do. Take your pick from your favorite athlete, celebrity, scientist, inventor or just about any other category and you will see that these people succeeded because they focused on their strengths and mastered their crafts.

Lacking a plan and commitment

When you fail to plan, you also plan to fail. A good plan is integral to achieving goals and bridging the execution gap as it gives you direction and helps you stay on track. Not having a plan will have you running amok.

And without a plan, there can be no commitment. How many times have you started a diet on Monday and then given it up the very next day just because your co-worker brought in a box of donuts to work? You didn't want to offend her so you thought that you would just start over the next day.

Commitment is key to execution and without any you will keep getting derailed from pursuing your goals.

Not having a deadline

As you have seen previously, working within a timeframe establishes a sense of urgency and focus. This alone should be enough to get anyone going towards their goal. But if you do not give yourself a deadline and keep things open ended, then you are setting yourself up for failure. Open ended scenarios are an easy road to procrastination and pushing things to the back burner.

Giving up halfway

Of course if you give up when the going gets tough, you won't be reaching that goal. We all live in a world that seeks out instant gratification and when perseverance doesn't deliver, quitting is viewed as an acceptable option.

Too often people are seen jumping from one job to another or if they try a business and do not see results, they change their field and venture into a new one. In one way this indicates the inability to handle failure. In another it shows the lack of proper goal setting.

Often people may fail to reach their goals because they do not know how to handle failure. They either choose to give up or change their goals when they face problems or do not get quick results.

Another consideration that factors into giving up is distraction. After setting up a goal, you may get distracted as other things come along making you neglect or even forget about your initial goal.

Chapter 8

Overcoming the Fear of Failure

"Failure is simply the opportunity to begin again, this time more intelligently" - Henry Ford

With so much talk about why good strategies fail or why certain goals are never achieved, you may think that you have covered everything about unaccomplished goals. However, the biggest hurdle that stops people from pursuing their goals is the fear of failure.

Having said that, failing to achieve goals does not mean that you have failed. It only implies that something may be wrong with your strategy and that you need to tweak it a bit. All you need to do is change your approach and change the way you do things.

The fear of failure can easily undermine your own efforts to avoid the possibility of a larger failure, immobilizing you and causing you to do nothing. This way your vision never gets translated into execution.

For some, the fear of failure can present such a powerful threat that their impulse to *avoid* failure exceeds their incentive to *succeed.*

What is failure?

Everyone has a different definition of failure given their individual benchmarks and values. It is a feeling of reluctance that stops a person from trying new things or getting involved in challenging projects.

In terms of setting goals and following through, fear of failure can sabotage all efforts. It can lead to procrastination, excessive anxiety or even perfectionism where you are only willing to try those things that you know you will finish perfectly and successfully.

It is almost impossible to go through life without experiencing some kind of failure but it is up to you to frame how you define your failure. Those who give up never follow their goals but others who view it as a learning experience pick up the pieces and proceed with getting to their goals.

How not to be afraid of failure

Before you set any aspirations or goals for yourself, know that things may not always go as planned. But you cannot let this uncertainty stop you from taking a chance. Instead, set yourself up for success by having a great vision and then a solid plan to back it up. Some ways that you can reduce the fear of failing can include the following:

Analyze all potential outcomes

Many people experience a fear of failure because they fear the unknown. This can stop you or make you uncomfortable from setting goals.

It is always better to have a contingency plan that can take you through. That may mean changing your strategy slightly but at least this way you have something to fall back on and keep moving forward.

Sometimes dividing your goals into smaller milestones can help. For instance, if your goal is to return to school to pursue your degree, start off by making sure you have the requisites in hand. Take care of any upgrades you need to pursue studies. Organize your finances, check out admission dates and locations and then go get that application form to fill out.

Taking one small step at a time will help build your confidence keeping you moving forward and prevent you from getting overwhelmed. It is important to realize that failure is about outcomes and results and not a personality trait.

Take action

By now you knowing that it's all about taking action. Action gives you the power to change the circumstances or the situation. If one strategy fails to produce results, do things differently. Instead, most people stop doing anything at all.

In this situation, persistence is key to achieving your goals. Instead of giving up, treat the experience as an opportunity to learn. Present yourself with questions like where you made the mistake, why it happened, how it could have been prevented and what else could you do to achieve your goals.

In essence, failure is feedback telling you that something is not working and that you need to change it. Perhaps one of the most well-known quotes about failure and the realization for change is by Steve Jobs:

"Getting fired from Apple was the best thing that could have ever happened to me. The heaviness of being successful was replaced by the lightness of being a beginner again, less sure about everything. It freed me to enter one of the most creative periods of my life."

Get away for a while

To get over your fear of failing, sometimes it is just better to take a break. This does not mean that you give up on your goals but simply that you redirect your focus elsewhere-temporarily.

The point is to clear your mind so you can see the bigger picture. Taking a break will also give you some time to think before your revisit you goal again. This time may also just give you enough compelling reason to act. So you reboot and restart.

Take the simple example of any software in your device. All software needs updating from time to time. Once updated, you will probably need to restart the device.

Likewise, you also need to reboot and restart after having faced some kind of setback. If you feel that your goal was unrealistic in some way, don't change the goal entirely. Instead look for a different strategy to get you to that goal. Maybe you need to extend the time frame for achieving that goal or perhaps you need to work on a specific aspect of improving your skill set to achieve that goal.

Let's refer back to an earlier example of trying to establish your blog. You may be writing great content but may also be missing out on the marketing component. To get good readership you need to learn how to market your blog. Re-approaching your goal, you may now want to spread the word so that others know about your blog's existence.

On an optimistic note, failure is the mother of all success. It often serves as a catapult to boost people to become successful and achieve their goals.

CONCLUSION

Now that you have come full circle by learning all there is to know about goal setting, achieving your goals and handling any hurdles that come along the way, we hope that you can put this information to the test.

On a parting note, just remember that goals are a way to measure your personal or professional success, giving you direction and focus. So go after your goals fully prepared and blow everyone else away.

Printed by Libri Plureos GmbH in Hamburg, Germany